Dear Parent:

Your child's love of reading starts here!

Every child learns to read in a different way and at his or her own speed. Some go back and forth between reading levels and read favorite books again and again. Others read through each level in order. You can help your young reader improve and become more confident by encouraging his or her own interests and abilities. From books your child reads with you to the first books he or she reads alone, there are I Can Read Books for every stage of reading:

SHARED READING
Basic language, word repetition, and whimsical illustrations, ideal for sharing with your emergent reader

BEGINNING READING
Short sentences, familiar words, and simple concepts for children eager to read on their own

READING WITH HELP
Engaging stories, longer sentences, and language play for developing readers

READING ALONE
Complex plots, challenging vocabulary, and high-interest topics for the independent reader

I Can Read Books have introduced children to the joy of reading since 1957. Featuring award-winning authors and illustrators and a fabulous cast of beloved characters, I Can Read Books set the standard for beginning readers.

A lifetime of discovery begins with the magical words "I Can Read!"

Visit www.icanread.com for information
on enriching your child's reading experience.

Do you sometimes stand on one leg, just for fun?
Then this book is for you!
—J.B.

The National Wildlife Federation & Ranger Rick contributors: Children's
Publication Staff, Licensing Staff, and in-house naturalist David Mizejewski

Ranger Rick: I Wish I Was a Flamingo
Copyright © 2021 National Wildlife Federation
All rights reserved.
Printed in the United States of America. No part of this book may be used or reproduced in any manner
whatsoever without written permission except in the case of brief quotations embodied in critical articles and
reviews. For information address HarperCollins Children's Books, a division of HarperCollins Publishers,
195 Broadway, New York, NY 10007.
www.icanread.com
www.RangerRick.com

Library of Congress Control Number: 2020937194
ISBN 978-0-06-243235-3 (trade bg) — ISBN 978-0-06-243234-6 (pbk.)

20 21 22 23 24 LSCC 10 9 8 7 6 5 4 3 2 1 ❖ First Edition

Ranger Rick

I Wish I Was a Flamingo

by Jennifer Bové

HARPER

An Imprint of HarperCollins Publishers

What if you wished you were a flamingo?

Then you became a flamingo!

Could you eat like a flamingo?

Talk like a flamingo?

Grow up in a flamingo family?

And would you want to? Find out!

Where would you live?

Flamingos are pink birds.

They have long, skinny legs.

Flamingos live in shallow lakes

called lagoons.

American flamingos live
in parts of Florida
as well as Central and South America
and in the Caribbean.

Flamingos walk around lagoons on their long legs.

They are almost always in the water.

Do you like to spend time in the water?

Flamingos eat in the water.

They talk to friends in the water.

They even lay their eggs in nests

surrounded by water!

How would your life begin?

These mud piles are flamingo nests.

There is one egg in each nest,

and one flamingo chick in each egg.

After hatching from its egg,
a chick stays in the nest
for a few days.

What would your family be like?

A flamingo mother and father
care for their chick.
They take turns feeding it.
The parents feed the chick a liquid
they make inside their throats.
The red liquid is called crop-milk.
They spit it into the chick's bill.

The chick leaves its muddy nest
after about a week.

The chick stretches its little legs and starts exploring the lagoon.

Do you mind getting muddy?

After a few more weeks,
all the flamingo chicks
in the lagoon
gather in a big group.
This group is called
a crèche (KRESH).
The chicks in a crèche
practice finding food
without their parents' help.

How would you learn to be a flamingo?

Flamingo chicks practice finding food like the grown-ups in their crèche.

The chicks learn to stir up mud
on the bottom of the lagoon
with their feet.
There is food in the mud.

What would you eat?

When a flamingo stirs up mud,
it also stirs up food to eat.
Flamingo feathers turn pink
because of a pink substance
in the plants and shrimp they eat.

How would you talk?

Flamingos are noisy birds.
They talk with honking, grunting,
and growling sounds.

22

Flamingos know each other's voices.
A flamingo chick can hear
its parents calling to it,
even in a crowded crèche.

Is your family noisy?

Where would you sleep?

When a flamingo feels sleepy,
it tucks its head under its wing.
Usually the bird sleeps standing up.

Sometimes, a flamingo sleeps while standing on just one leg!

How would growing up change you?

As a flamingo chick grows up, its bill gets much bigger. Its neck and legs grow longer.

How have you changed since you've gotten older?

The chick's gray feathers turn pink
as it eats more and more food.

Being a flamingo could be cool.

But do you want to play in the mud?

Live with lots of other flamingos?

Stand on one leg while you sleep?

Luckily, you don't have to.

You're not a flamingo.

You're YOU!

Did You Know?

* The flamingos in this book are American flamingos. There are five other kinds of flamingos that live around the world. They all look a lot alike.

* The American flamingo is about five feet tall.

* Flamingos do a lot of walking, but they can fly, too. Sometimes, they fly long distances.

* Flamingos can live up to 60 years.

* Flamingo feathers turn pink because of a pink substance in the plants and shrimp they eat.

Make Pink Ink

Flamingo feathers turn pink because of substances in the shrimp they eat called carotenoids. Carotenoids are also in some vegetables we eat, like carrots and beets. You can use these veggies to make pink ink.

With a grown-up's help, blend up a carrot and a beet in a blender with one cup of water.

Pour the juicy blend into a bowl. Notice how brightly colored it is—that's the carotenoid!

Dip a clean, dry sponge into the bowl to soak up the juice. Put the sponge on a paper plate. Using this ink sponge, make Thumbprint Flamingos. There are instructions on Ranger Rick's website (RangerRick.org/crafts_activities/thumbprint -flamingos).

Your flamingos will be colored with the same substance as real flamingos!

Wild Words

Bill: a bird's beak, which is both its mouth and nose

Crèche: a group of flamingo chicks

Crop-milk: a liquid that mother and father flamingos make in their throats to feed to their chick

Flamingo: a pink bird that lives in lagoons around the world

Lagoon: a shallow lake full of salty water

Dig Deeper

WANT TO FIND OUT EVEN MORE ABOUT FLAMINGOS?

Check out the Ranger Rick website: www.RangerRick.com SEARCH: flamingo

Photography © Getty Images by saurabh13, USO, Photo by Steve Wilson, Nils Hastrup/500px, Gunnar Mallon, Javier Fernández Sánchez, DejaVu Designs, photo by yasa, Federico Mas, Vicki Jauron, Babylon and Beyond Photography, chuvipro, emarys, VladimSu, jorgeabohorquez, ANDREYGUDKOV, k02, photo168, ZU_09, Anup Shah